HOMEMADE
HOLIDAY

HOMEMADE
HOLIDAY

Sophie Pester
Catharina Bruns

Contents

"A festival of joy and friendship it shall be. Because friendship is the finest gift a person can give."

Author unknown

Introduction

'Tis the season once more! As the first advent lights are lit, it's time to turn your thoughts and fingers to making the Christmas festivities at home truly special for you and your friends and family.

This unique winter festival is a time for contemplation and togetherness, but also a celebration of special wishes, gifts, and presents. That is probably why Christmas is such a great time to be creative; there is no better way to express your love and affection than with homemade gifts and personalized decorations. As you will see, the yuletide spirit can be created in just a few easy steps. What would Christmas be without the familiar evocative aromas, the festive ornaments, and the twinkling eyes of excited children having fun?

This book is crammed with wonderful ideas for a creative Christmas: from DIY decorations and gifts, to imaginative gift-wrapping ideas, and super-quick, last-minute projects. Because—quite honestly—who has time to spare at this time of year? To guarantee a festive mood without the preparations degenerating into a total stress meltdown, we have been particularly careful to design the projects here to be simple to achieve while still being impressive. Most are not too time-consuming and can be made over the Christmas period with materials you may well already have tucked away in closets at home. We want to inspire you to make lovely little offerings for your friends and family, and to conjure up a relaxed and beautiful holiday by getting in touch with your inner creative spirit. Many of the crafting ideas in the book can also be made with children. After all, the most important thing at Christmas is to find time for each other and to make things nice and cozy!

Wishing you a wonderful Christmas,

Sophie & Catharina

Basic equipment

Whatever the craft activity, having the correct tools is half the battle! To make sure the projects in this book run smoothly and turn out well, here is a brief list of materials you may need.

We have made sure our projects can be achieved without expensive or unusual tools. The equipment used is generally found in any creative household or, if not, is widely available in stores. As a crafting enthusiast, you will probably already own much of it.

The following will set you up to take on any of the craft ideas in this book:

* scissors
* pens
* calligraphy pen
* craft glue and glue stick
* adhesive tape and masking tape
* various paintbrushes
* acrylic paints
* wire
* little sponges
* thread and sewing machine
* cord, yarn, and embroidery threads
* sewing and embroidery needles
* crochet hooks and knitting needles
* pins
* iron
* nail polish
* hole punch
* pliers
* cutting board
* ruler (with steel edge)
* craft knife or cutter
* glue gun
* linoleum cutters
* linoleum ink roller

✷ Tip ✷

You can tell how difficult a project is by the number of little stars above the list of materials. One star means it is super easy; for three stars, you will need a bit more time.

Decorating

· · · · · · · · · · · · · ⬤ · · · · · · · · · · · · ·

*Festive ornaments are as much a part
of Christmas as candy canes and Santa
Claus. Creative decorative projects
are fun, and will get you in the
yuletide mood as you work...*

Marbled tree ornaments

Every Christmas the same question crops up—what color scheme should we choose for the tree decorations? This year, you can create your own customized combination.

Bespoke ball ornaments are absolutely perfect if you are looking for Christmas tree decorations that will stand out from the classic red, but are unusual while still being festive and fashionable. They are quick to make and, of course, you can choose whatever colors your heart desires.

How it's done:

1. Attach a piece of string to a Christmas ball ornament. Fill a large bowl with enough lukewarm water to completely submerge the ball.

2. Add a few drops from each of the bottles of nail polish to the water. The nail polish will form a thin, colorful film on the surface of the water.

3. Now immerse the ball completely in the bowl, holding the cap and ring to push it under water.

4. A thin layer of nail polish will coat the ball. Hang it up to dry for a couple of hours.

❋ ❋ ❋

🕐 *2 minutes per ornament, plus drying time*

You will need:

∗ *colorful thread or string*
∗ *scissors*
∗ *white Christmas tree ball ornaments in various sizes*
∗ *large bowl*
∗ *nail polish in 2 colors, here: orange and lilac*

Evergreen garland

This string of Christmas lights is a very festive project, using fragrant coniferous branches and tree ornaments.

∗❄❄

🕐 1–2 hours

You will need:

∗ scissors
∗ evergreen branches
∗ long chain of small Christmas lights on green wire
∗ green thread or wire
∗ Christmas tree decorations

If you don't like the idea of having a Christmas tree, or don't have space for one, you can make yourself a beautiful alternative with this garland. It is guaranteed to create a celebratory atmosphere and can be hung up around a doorway. The presents will feel quite at home underneath!

How it's done:

1. Cut individual offshoots from the evergreen branches and attach them to the Christmas lights using little pieces of thread or wire. Try to leave no gaps; the lights should seem to be shining out from a garland of pine twigs.

2. Now hang up the chain, attaching it securely to a door frame, to a fireplace, or to another chosen spot.

3. Finally, decorate the garland with Christmas tree decorations, such as ball ornaments and stars.

∗ Tip ∗

By using outdoor Christmas lights and weatherproof decorations, you can also use this idea to adorn your balcony or yard.

Festive floral ball

This beautiful ornament works both inside and in a sheltered spot outdoors, and you don't need to be a florist to make it.

These lush green orbs are easy to make and are a quick way of embellishing any room. If you dampen the floral foam, the plants will stay fresh for longer. Use any festive greenery you have; those listed here are just suggestions.

How it's done:

1. Lay out a 5ft (160cm) length of wire, then double it up. Push this, loop first, all the way through a foam ball.

2. Bend and twist the wire loop to create a hook. This will enable you to hang up your ornament later.

∗∗❄

🕙 *1 hour per sphere*

You will need:

* *thick gold-colored wire*
* *2 floral foam bulls, 4in (10cm) and 6in (15cm) in diameter*
* *scissors*
* *eucalyptus branches*
* *sea holly (Eryngium planum)*
* *St. John's wort with berries*
* *ivy berries*
* *false cypress (Chamaccyparis) branches*
* *florist greening pins*
* *little gold bells*
* *pins with flat metal heads*

Warning:

Many berries are poisonous and can be left out or replaced by other plant varieties, if you prefer.

3. Cut your chosen twigs, flowers, and berries into little pieces. Attach greening pins to the little gold bells. Poke all the pieces into the ball all the way around. Start with the greenery, fixing a few of the larger leaves in place with pins so they don't stick out too much, then distribute the flowers, berries, and bells in between. Hang using the hook or the long ends of the wire.

Winter wreath

You can make a floral wreath from baby's breath (gypsophila) in no time at all. It looks fantastic hanging in a modern home and conjures up a wintry mood, even if you prefer your Christmas decorations on the minimalist side.

∗ ❄ ❄
🕓 *30 minutes*

You will need:
∗ *scissors*
∗ *baby's breath (gypsophila)*
∗ *white metal ring, 8–12in (20–30cm) in diameter*
∗ *thin wire*
∗ *ribbon, for hanging*

Baby's breath is really easy to work with, and the wreath will look great even without any additional decorative elements. Of course, if you like, you can spruce it up a bit more with little balls or bells.

How it's done:

1. Cut little offshoots from the baby's breath, then take 1 or 2 of these together, lay the stems along the metal ring, and wrap thin wire around them 3–4 times.

2. Continue attaching flower sprigs until the entire ring is covered, erring on the side of generosity and leaving no gaps.

3. Securely hang the wreath up in your chosen spot with a length of ribbon.

∗ **Tip** ∗

Baby's breath still looks good when it has dried out, so the wreath can happily stay hanging in your home for a long time.

Christmas potpourri

One of the best things about the festive period is the scents that waft through your house, whether from baking cookies, pine needles, peppermint, or Christmas spices like cinnamon.

This natural room fragrance adds immeasurably to the anticipation of Christmas and creates a homey atmosphere. An aromatic decoration for a cosy time of year.

How it's done:

1. When you next go on a woodland walk, bring home a couple of lovely evergreen sprigs and some pinecones and put them in a large bowl. If there is some resin coming out of the sprigs and cones, all the better. The resin contains particularly high quantities of essential oils and has a wonderful coniferous aroma. Add a couple of little yuletide logs, too, if you like.

2. The perfect partners for these fresh woody scents are oranges, mandarins, lemons, apples, cinnamon sticks, and walnuts. A particularly special addition to the festive fragrances can be created by including a bergamot orange, if you can find one. This is a citrus fruit that tea drinkers may be familiar with: Earl Grey tea is flavored with bergamot oil. To help release the scent of the bergamot, carefully carve shallow incisions in the rind using a knife.

∗ ❋ ❋
⏲ *10 minutes*

You will need:
∗ *evergreen sprigs*
∗ *pinecones*
∗ *large bowl*
∗ *logs (optional)*
∗ *oranges*
∗ *mandarins*
∗ *lemons*
∗ *apples*
∗ *cinnamon sticks*
∗ *walnuts*
∗ *bergamot orange (optional)*
∗ *knife (optional)*

∗ Tip ∗

The mandarins, apples, oranges, and walnuts can be eaten straight from the bowl over the festive period.

Dried flower advent wreath

If you are not a fan of traditional advent wreaths, this alternative, understated option might be the perfect solution for you.

✳ ✳ ❋

🕐 *30 minutes*

You will need:

✳ *scissors*
✳ *hydrangea flowers, fresh or dried*
✳ *floral foam ring with waterproof base, 16–20in (40–50cm) in diameter*
✳ *4 white candles*

"Thousands of candles can be lit from a single candle, and the life of the single candle will not be shortened. Happiness never decreases by being shared."

Buddha

It's incredibly easy to make this wonderful wreath using dried hydrangea flowers. The advent candles are simply positioned in the middle. When advent is over, the wreath can still be used as a decoration. It keeps for a long time and is a beautiful addition to your coffee table, or hung on a wall.

How it's done:

1. Depending on their size, cut the flower heads to create smaller bunches. Stick these bunches into the foam ring. Continue until you've completely covered the ring. Finally, place the candles in the center of your wreath.

2. We made our wreath from flowers that we picked in the fall and dried ourselves. If you want to use fresh flowers, you can soak the foam ring in water beforehand. Later it can just be left standing, without needing more water, and the arrangement will slowly dry out over time—the flowers will still look amazing.

Christmas tree garlands

Didn't there used to be more tinsel?
Yes... but these days we want some fresh ideas
for the Christmas tree.

These fun garlands made from beads, bells, and popcorn are perfect if you want a natural look for your tree. Threading the garlands is a guaranteed evening of fun for the whole family. Just be careful when you're piercing the popcorn… and don't gobble up all your working materials.

How it's done:

1. For each chain, cut a 6½ft (2m) piece of string.

2. Use the needle to thread popcorn, beads, pom-poms, and bells, in whatever order you choose. You can also make the garland from a single material, like the pom-pom garland at the bottom of the tree in the picture on the left. Don't use freshly made popcorn because it crumbles and is really tricky to thread. Leftover popcorn from a previous evening's movie viewing is perfect!

∗ ❄ ❄

🕐 *30 minutes per garland*

You will need:

* ∗ *scissors*
* ∗ *string or thread*
* ∗ *thin needle*
* ∗ *salted popcorn (a few days old)*
* ∗ *beads*
* ∗ *white pom-poms in various sizes*
* ∗ *little bells*

Snowflake tablecloth

Even if today's Christmas celebrations have been modernized, we still like to be reminded of the old traditions.

One of those long-established customs is the Christmas tablecloth, sewed by great-grandma and handed down through the generations. So we had to give this book a similar project. An embroidered tablecloth is a wonderful "forever" heirloom that children, grandchildren, and great-grandchildren will still be able to enjoy for years to come.

How it's done:

1. First transfer the embroidery design on to the tablecloth. To do this, poke through the holes in the template on to the fabric with a pencil or transfer pen (follow the marker package instructions for use). If you sketch the design first with a transfer pen, the pattern can be removed later with cold water.

2. Next, connect the individual pre-sketched points using simple stitches (see pp108–109).

★ ★ ❄

🕐 *depending on the size of the tablecloth, the design, and your level of diligence, 5 hours to 50 years*

You will need:

* ★ *template (see p122)*
* ★ *white cotton or linen tablecloth*
* ★ *sharp pencil, or transfer pen*
* ★ *white embroidery thread*
* ★ *embroidery needle*
* ★ *scissors*

Did you know that, in Poland, the Christmas dinner table is always laid with an extra place setting? This is a sign of hospitality. It means that an unexpected guest will always have a seat at the table.

Pom-pom door wreath

Yarn pom-poms and tassels lend a dash of warmth and color to this characterful door decoration.

✱✱❋

🕐 *1 hour*

You will need:

* *evergreen sprigs (such as pine)*
* *willow wreath*
* *wire*
* *small pinecones*
* *glue gun*
* *yarn, here: red and pink*
* *scissors*
* *moss*

✱ Tip ✱

When Christmas is over, you can remove all the materials from the wreath and either save them for next year or redecorate the wreath at Easter.

To make this pretty wreath, you just need a willow wreath that you can adorn in a festive manner with colorful pom-poms, sprigs, and pinecones. As an added bonus, this is a great way of using up leftover bits of yarn. It looks fantastic, and all your visitors will immediately want their own.

How it's done:

1. Attach the sprigs to the willow wreath using wire. Stick the cones in place using the glue gun. Add a touch of personality by making a couple of red and pink pom-poms (see p121) in different sizes, then use the glue gun again to attach these to the wreath.

2. Pick slender pieces of moss, wrap them around with wire, and attach these little rolls to the wreath.

3. Finally, make two tassels (see p121) and hang them at different heights below the wreath.

0

Christmas tree decorations

Painted wood decorations

These pretty Christmas tree decorations are quick to make and far more attractive than many store-bought trinkets.

You can buy ready-cut, natural wooden discs from craft supplies stores, and then they just need to be painted. Adding a personal touch to this year's Christmas decorations is easier than you think.

How it's done:

1. First drill a little hole about ¼in (5mm) from the edge of each disc for hanging them later.

2. Now mix a bit of white acrylic paint with water to get a very thin consistency and glaze the wooden disc with it. The grain of the wood should remain visible, the color is just a bit lighter. Let the glaze dry thoroughly.

3. Now you can paint both sides of the wooden disc in whatever way you like, using red paint or the silver marker. Use the star template to help you, or paint cheerful Santa faces or patterns on to the wooden discs. Once they are dry, pass the red thread through the holes to hang up your decorations.

✱✱❄

🕐 *5 minutes per decoration, plus drying time*

You will need:

* *drill and ⅛in (3mm) diameter drill bit*
* *wooden discs, 2–2½in (5–6cm) in diameter*
* *white and red acrylic paint*
* *thin flat paintbrush*
* *silver marker*
* *template (see p122)*
* *red thread*
* *scissors*

②

Christmas tree decorations

Lebkuchen hearts

These are a classic German tradition and should be on every Christmas tree! Nibbling is positively encouraged.

✱✱❋

🕐 *2 hours, plus cooling time*

You will need:

For the cookies:
* *7 tbsp (150g) honey*
* *⅓ cup (75g) superfine sugar*
* *3½ tbsp (50g) unsalted butter*
* *1 tbsp cocoa powder*
* *½ cup (50g) ground almonds*
* *1 tsp lebkuchen spice mix, from German stores or online*
* *1 small egg, lightly beaten*
* *pinch of salt*
* *2¼ cups (275g) all-purpose flour*
* *2 tsp baking powder*

In addition:
* *baking sheet*
* *parchment paper*
* *saucepan*
* *rolling pin*
* *heart-shaped cookie cutter*
* *wide straw*
* *½ cup (200g) chocolate ganache sauce, from cooking stores or online*
* *double boiler*
* *handful of blanched almonds*
* *frying pan*
* *cooling rack*
* *thin ribbon*

How it's done:

1. Preheat the oven to 400°F (200°C) and line a cookie sheet with parchment paper. Heat the honey, sugar, and butter in a saucepan until the sugar dissolves.

2. Leave the mixture to cool slightly, then stir in the cocoa, ground almonds, spices, egg, and salt. Next add the flour and baking powder and mix until you have a smooth dough.

3. Roll out the dough until it is about ¼in (5mm) thick and cut out hearts. In the upper center of each heart, use a wide straw to punch a hole in the dough. Lay the hearts on the prepared sheet and bake for 10–12 minutes, then leave to cool.

4. Heat the chocolate ganache over a double boiler according to the package instructions until it has melted.

5. Halve the almonds lengthwise and toast them gently in a dry frying pan.

6. Put the hearts on a cooling rack, coat with the ganache, and press 2 almond halves into the ganache. As soon as the ganache has hardened, you can hang the hearts on your Christmas tree with thin ribbon.

*The custom of having a tree in your home and decorating
it at Christmas time has been around for hundreds of years.
The evergreen tree is a reminder of new life during the dark
winter months, while lit candles are a symbol of hope.*

Winter night dream catcher

These atmospheric rings are a lovely idea for a gift, or for decorating bedrooms, especially children's rooms.

These are just right for this time of contemplation and help bring sweet dreams to overstimulated minds, particularly for children at Christmas! You can hang a little angel or other festive symbol inside the ring.

How it's done:

1. For the first ring, tweak a metal ring open with pliers. Now thread the wooden beads on to the ring and tie 4 short strands of yarn between each. To do this, double the yarn over, slip the loop under the ring, then take both yarn ends over the ring and through the loop. Next pull the loop firm and cut the yarn ends to the same length. As soon as the ring has been completely adorned with beads and yarn, close it again with a little piece of tape and push the decorations over the join.

2. For the second ring, knot the different colored yarns next to each other on the ring. You can tie them together, braid them, or hang beads on them. To finish off, you can hang a Christmas tree decoration inside the ring.

3. For the third ring, tie longer strands of yarn on to the ring and use a yarn needle to thread beads on to them. End each string with a golden bead and secure it with a knot. The stepped shape is created by hanging either an extra bead or a bead less to each strand of yarn as you progress along the ring.

✳ ✳ ✳

🕐 *30 minutes per ring*

You will need:
* ✱ *3 white metal rings: 1 × 6in (15cm) and 2 × 8in (20cm) in diameter*
* ✱ *universal pliers*
* ✱ *wooden beads, ½in (1cm) and ¾in (1.5cm) in diameter*
* ✱ *yarn in shades of white, tan, and gray*
* ✱ *scissors*
* ✱ *adhesive tape*
* ✱ *Christmas tree decorations*
* ✱ *yarn needle*
* ✱ *golden glass beads, ¼–½in (5–10mm) in diameter*

"When you dream, you should set no limits."

Honoré de Balzac

Giving

🎁

*Christmas means presents and, in
our world, presents mean creativity.
Homemade gifts are always special.
In this chapter we will inspire you
with a wealth of clever ideas that are
both quick to make and guaranteed
to bring joy to your loved ones.*

Advent calendar

This lovely idea has a bag for every day of December up to Christmas Eve. It is destined to be a lifelong companion—reused every year, or handed down to younger siblings.

Use a stamp to print little motifs on the individual advent calendar pouches, which you can then hang up where you choose. This delightful calendar is easy to make and offers enough room for 24 little treats and presents. And, once Christmas is over, you can store it away in a pretty bag for next year.

How it's done:

1. First cut out the copied templates.

2. Now transfer the shapes and numbers onto the foam and cut them all out.

3. Stick the motif on the outside of a transparent CD case. (After stamping you can peel it off again and stick on another one, so you don't need a new CD case for every motif.)

4. Use a little sponge to dab some fabric dye of your choice onto the foam until the entire surface is evenly covered. ➥➥

* ❋ ❋
◔ *3–4 hours*

You will need:

* ✳ *templates (see pp123–125)*
* ✳ *pen*
* ✳ *scissors*
* ✳ *self-adhesive foam*
* ✳ *old CD cases*
* ✳ *little sponges*
* ✳ *fabric dye in red, blue, yellow, and green*
* ✳ *newspaper*
* ✳ *12 cotton bags, about 6 × 4in (15 × 10cm)*
* ✳ *12 cotton bags, about 8 × 6in (20 × 15cm)*
* ✳ *iron*
* ✳ *needle and thread*
* ✳ *24 bells*
* ✳ *1 large fabric bag, about 16 × 12in (40 × 30cm)*

5. Lay some newspaper inside the cotton bags to stop the dye from coming through both layers, then stamp the foam shape onto the material. On the back of the bag, stamp one of the numbers between 1 and 24.

6. Allow the fabric dye to dry, and then fix it according to the package instructions with the iron.

7. Finally, sew a bell onto each of the bottom corners of the large cotton bags.

8. On the large fabric bag, you can print the name of the future owner, plus various motifs. This bag can be used to store the advent calendar between Christmases.

* Tip *

Stamp different motifs one after another with the same color, so you don't need to wash out the sponge every time.

🎁

*The origins of the advent calendar can be traced back to the 19th century.
The first advent calendars consisted of 24 little pictures with Christmas
designs, which would be hung up individually on each day. Alternatively,
people simply drew 24 chalk marks on the wall, one of which was wiped
away each day, to show how many days were left until Christmas.*

Good luck angel

Not only is this angel really attractive, it also has a very special place at Christmas.

From its position at the window or on a door, it listens closely to what the people who live in the home want for Christmas, and also protects the family from conflict and upset during the festive season.

How it's done:

★★❄

⊕ *1–2 hours*

You will need:

* ★ *9 × 12in craft felt sheets in red and pink*
* ★ *templates (see p126)*
* ★ *pen*
* ★ *scissors*
* ★ *needle*
* ★ *red and gold thread*
* ★ *polyfill*
* ★ *⅛in (2mm) beads in pale blue, pink, and yellow*
* ★ *various larger beads*
* ★ *golden bell*

1. Fold the red craft felt in half along its width, lay the cut out template on it, and trace the outline. The straight edge should be lined up flush with the folded-over edge of the fabric. Then cut out the angel.

2. Sew up the sides using a buttonhole stitch (see p107), leaving an opening of about 2in (5cm), then stuff the angel with the polyfill. Finally, sew up the opening.

3. Cut out the crown from the pink felt and sew it to the head using a running stitch (see p108). Decorate the crown and robe with beads. Sew tassels (see p121) made from gold thread onto the corners of the skirt.

4. Finally, thread a short string of beads and the bell and sew it centrally to the bottom edge of the angel. Attach a thin thread to the angel's head to hang it up.

Soap diamonds

This fun project isn't just for Christmas. If you make enough, it should provide a wonderfully fragrant reminder of your gift all year round.

✶❋❋

🕐 *15 minutes, plus drying time*

You will need:

✶ *large saucepan*
✶ *small saucepan, or heatproof bowl*
✶ *raw soap, transparent and white*
✶ *diamond-shaped silicone mold*

These little crystal-shaped soaps are quick to make and can be enriched with various scents, or combined with herb leaves and flower petals.

How it's done:

1. Heat some water in a large saucepan. Then suspend a smaller saucepan or heatproof bowl over the larger one, add the raw soap, and melt it in this double boiler.

2. When the raw soap has completely melted, pour it into a silicone mold and put it in a cool place. After about 1 hour, the soap will have solidified and you can release the individual pieces from the mold.

"A true gift is something you offer to someone else that you would rather have kept for yourself."

Selma Lagerlöf

✶ Tip ✶

You can add fragrance to the soap by using an essential oil of your choice. Just add a couple of drops of oil to the liquid soap before you pour it into the mold.

❶
Cosmetic bags
Striped bag

This is a lovely gift for anyone who needs to stash their toiletries safely when traveling. Tips and tricks for knitting can be found from page 110.

How it's done:

1. The bag is knitted completely in garter stitch (see p112). Loosely cast on 27 stitches in blue.

2. Work the 1st row in blue, then 2 rows in white (with yarn doubled), then 2 rows in blue.

3. Continue in these alternating colors. Finish when the piece measures about 10in (25cm) ending on a blue row, and cast off loosely on the reverse side. The knitted piece should measure about 10 × 8in (26 × 20cm).

4. Fold the knitted piece in half with the wrong side facing outward. Sew up the side seams and sew in all the loose ends.

5. Turn the bag right side out. The pouch should now measure about 8 × 5in (20 × 13cm).

6. Finally, prepare and insert the bag lining and zipper (see p49).

🎁

"The more we make other people happy, the more joy we receive in our own heart in return."

Traditional proverb

✱✱✱
🕑 *3–4 hours*

You will need:
For the knitted bag:
* ✱ 24in (60cm) 10.5mm (UK size 3) circular needle
* ✱ about 32yd superbulky blue yarn, here: Lamana Nazca (40% alpaca, 40% merino, 20% nylon)
* ✱ about 32yd DK-weight white yarn, here: Lamana Cusco (100% alpaca), knitted with the yarn held double
* ✱ 1 yarn needle
* ✱ scissors

For the lining:
* ✱ 14 × 10in (35 × 25cm) fabric
* ✱ blue thread
* ✱ 7in (18cm) long colorful zipper
* ✱ needle
* ✱ pins
* ✱ sewing machine

②

Cosmetic bags

Two-tone bag

*Whether for cosmetics, pens, or loose change,
this pretty wool bag is a must.*

How it's done:

1. Loosely cast on 27 stitches in white (with the yarn held double).

2. Knit 6 rows in moss stitch (see p114).

3. On the 7th row, knit 2, then, from the doubled yarn, knit 1 stitch from the first strand and another stitch from the second strand (so 2 knit stitches are created from a single stitch), then continue with knit 1, knit 2 stitches from 1, knit 1, knit 2 stitches from 1, to the end of the row, finishing with an edge stitch. (39 stitches)

4. Switch to anthracite: knit 1 stitch, purl to the last stitch, then knit the last stitch. Continue in stockinette stitch.

5. When the piece measures about 8½in (21cm), switch to white on a right side row: knit 1, *1 knit stitch, knit 2 together, repeat from * to the last 2 stitches, then knit 2. (27 stitches)

6. Then work a further 6 rows in moss stitch and cast off loosely on row 7.

7. Measure your knitted piece. The white upper and lower edges should be about 8½in (21cm) wide, and the middle section in anthracite about 11½in (29cm) wide. Thanks to the increases and decreases at the color transition, the knitted piece is convex in shape. You will need to take this into account when cutting the lining fabric to size.

8. Fold the knitting in half with the wrong side facing out. Sew up the side seams and sew in all the loose ends.

9. Turn the bag right side out. The pouch should now be about 11½in (29cm) wide at the bottom, 8½in (21cm) wide at the top, and about 5½in (14cm) tall. To prepare and insert the lining fabric, see opposite.

✱✱✱
🕙 *3–4 hours*

You will need:
For the knitted bag:
✱ *20in (50cm) 7mm (UK size 2) circular needle*
✱ *about 32yd DK-weight white yarn, here: Lamana Cusco (100% alpaca), knitted with the yarn held double*
✱ *about 64yd anthracite color superbulky yarn, here: Lamana Nazca (40% alpaca, 40% merino, 20% nylon)*
✱ *1 yarn needle*
✱ *scissors*

For the lining:
✱ *paper pattern (see p127)*
✱ *14 × 14in (35 × 35cm) fabric*
✱ *7in (18cm) long colorful zipper*
✱ *pins*
✱ *sewing machine*
✱ *needle*
✱ *white thread*

Lining bag and finishing
How it's done:

The same approach is used for both designs.

For the striped bag, cut the fabric according to the dimensions of the knitted pouch, adding ½in (1cm) seam allowance at the sides. For the two-tone bag, use the template (see p127), and this time add a ¾in (2cm) seam allowance.

1. Pin the zipper onto the right side of the material along the short edge (the zipper pull should be on top) and sew the upper zipper tape in place with a sewing machine. Pin and sew the other edge in a similar manner.

2. Now sew up the side seams (using the seam allowance of ½in / 1cm), from the bottom all the way up to the zipper seam.

3. Place the lining bag inside the knitted bag. Pin the upper edges together, making sure that the side seams are aligned.

4. Hand sew the knitted bag to the zipper fastener using the needle and thread and making small adjustments as you go to avoid bunching.

Family T-shirts

Over Christmas not only are you allowed to slow down, but some real rest and recuperation—including hanging around in comfortable clothes—are positively encouraged.

With this in mind, we have designed comfy handmade outfits for the whole family, so you can look good (and festive) while you're sleeping in.

How it's done:

1. The T-shirts are all printed with the same design. We've varied the colors a bit. First, cut out the copied templates, transfer them to the foam, and cut them all out. Stick the motifs onto the outside of a transparent CD case.

2. Use the little sponge to dab a bit of your chosen fabric dye onto the foam until the entire surface is evenly covered.

3. Lay some newspaper inside the T-shirts to stop the dye from penetrating both layers, then stamp on the foam shapes. Leave the fabric dye to dry and then fix it according to the package instructions with the iron.

4. For the kid's T-shirt, we used a cotton swab to print red dots onto a Christmas tree, and also painted a smiley face on the tree.

* ⁂ ⁂

🕐 *15 minutes per shirt*

You will need:

* *templates (see p128)*
* *pen*
* *scissors*
* *self-adhesive foam*
* *old CD cases*
* *little sponge*
* *fabric dye in green, white, black, red, and yellow*
* *newspaper*
* *white T-shirts for the whole family*
* *iron*
* *cotton swabs*

⁎ Tip ⁎

If you prefer, design your own family Christmas motif and use that instead of our template.

Photo cube

Great for your shelves or bedside table.

∗❀❀

🕐 *30 minutes per cube*

You will need:

∗ *craft knife*
∗ *cutting mat*
∗ *ruler with a steel edge*
∗ *printed photos*
∗ *glue stick*
∗ *paper to use as underlay*
∗ *2 wooden cubes, 3in (7cm) and 4in (10cm)*

Shared memories are something to treasure. That's why this photo cube is the ideal present for close friends, family, or your partner. It doesn't take long to make and it is something really personal—so much more original and versatile than a traditional picture frame.

How it's done:

1. Cut your photos to shape. For our 3in (7cm) and 4in (10cm) cubes, we cut our pictures to measure 2½in² (6cm²) and 3½in² (9cm²).

2. Apply glue evenly over the back of the photos, laying some paper underneath to prevent your work surface from getting dirty.

3. Now stick the photos centrally on each side of the wooden cube.

❶
Cuddly star
Large crochet star

These adorable stars are designed as a gift for younger kids. They are perfect travel companions, or make a little friend for cuddling in bed.

How it's done:

Both stars are made in 2 sections using single crochet stitch. First you crochet from the center out in a spiral (which creates a slightly bulging shape), then you crochet the points of the star back and forth in rows. Tips and tricks for crocheting can be found from page 116.

1st round: crochet a 5 stitch loop.
2nd round: single crochet into every stitch. (10 stitches)
3rd round: single crochet into every 2nd stitch. (15 stitches)
4th round: single crochet into every 3rd stitch. (20 stitches)
5th round: single crochet into every 4th stitch. (25 stitches)
6th round: single crochet into every 5th stitch. (30 stitches)
7th round: single crochet into every 6th stitch. (35 stitches)
8th round: single crochet into every 7th stitch. (40 stitches)
9th round: single crochet into every 8th stitch. (45 stitches)
10th round: single crochet into every 9th stitch. (50 stitches)
11th round: single crochet into every 10th stitch. (55 stitches)
12th round: single crochet into every 11th stitch. (60 stitches)
13th round: single crochet into every 12th stitch. (65 stitches)
14th round: single crochet into every 13th stitch. (70 stitches)

Now you crochet the 5 points of the star in rows as follows (as you have 70 stiches, there will be 14 stitches for each point of the star):

1. For the 1st point of the star, single crochet 14 stitches (insert a stitch marker in the following stitch—this is where you will later start the 2nd point). Turn the work.

2. Next row: no turning chain stitch, skip 1 stitch, single crochet to the end of the row. Continue in this manner, decreasing 1 stitch per row, and the point will form nice and evenly. Finally, you are left with 1 stitch. Cut the thread and pull it through the loop. ➤➤

∗∗∗
🕐 *2–3 hours*

You will need:
* *4.5mm; G/6 (UK size 7) crochet hook*
* *about 186yd, 3½oz (100g) DK-weight yarn in gray or white, here: Lamana Cusco (100% alpaca)*
* *stitch marker*
* *scissors*
* *yarn needle*
* *about 1oz (30g) polyfill*
* *embroidery needle (optional)*
* *black yarn scraps (optional)*

Finished dimensions: about 9½in (24cm) in diameter

3. The 2nd point begins from the stitch marker. Remove the stitch marker, join in the yarn again here, and crochet a chain stitch (this counts as the first stitch). Single crochet a further 13 stitches up to the end of the row, turn the work, and crochet this point exactly as you did for the first. Work the remaining points in the same way.

4. Crochet the second side of the star as above.

5. Carefully sew up any loose threads on the wrong side (the interior) of both sections. Firmly pull the thread from the loop at the start and likewise sew in this end.

6. Lay the 2 sections with wrong sides facing and single crochet the edges of the points together. At the upper end of the points, single crochet 3 times into 1 stitch.

7. When only 2 edges are open, start stuffing in the polyfill—take small quantities of the polyfill and use the handle of your crochet hook to push these into the points of each star. Continue filling to the center, making sure this is particularly well stuffed.

8. For the 2 final edges, you will have to alternate between crocheting the seam together and inserting more polyfill. Cut the final thread and secure it well. Mold the star into shape. If you like, you can embroider a face with black yarn.

"It is Christmas in the heart that puts Christmas in the air."

William Turner Ellis

②

Cuddly star

Small crochet star

This smaller variant of the same star is an even cuter present for cuddling and playing with.

How it's done:

1. Work the small star up to and including the 10th row in exactly the same way as for the large star. After the 10th round, there are 50 stitches. Now the 5 points are crocheted in rows as follows (as you have 50 stiches, there will be 10 stitches for each point of the star):

2. For the 1st point, single crochet 10 stitches (insert a stitch marker in the next stitch; this is where you will later begin the 2nd point). Turn the work.

3. Next row—no turning chain stitch, skip 1 stitch, single crochet to the end of the row. Continue in this way, crocheting the first point as described for the large star.

4. The 2nd point begins from the stitch marker. Remove the stitch marker, join in the yarn again, and crochet a chain stitch (this counts as the first stitch). Single crochet a further 9 stitches to the end of the row, turn the work, and crochet as described above to the end.

5. Work the remaining points and the second half of the star as described for the large star. Similarly, crochet the 2 halves together and stuff the star.

***

🕐 *2–3 hours*

You will need:

* *4.5mm; G/6 (UK size 7) crochet hook*
* *about 93yd, 1¾oz (50g) pale blue or yellow DK-weight yarn: here Lamana Cusco (100% alpaca)*
* *stitch marker*
* *scissors*
* *yarn needle*
* *about ¾oz (20g) polyfill*

Finished dimensions: about 7in (18cm) in diameter

* Tip *

To help count your spiral rounds, mark the first stitch of each new round with a stitch marker.

Buchgestaltung in der Schweiz

Ascona-Presse erschien 1986
auf der Kniehebelpresse de
Antiqua des Ireneo Nicor
Presse, Josef Weiss, hat
stes, interessantes Pro
Eine Reihe von
Alice, Comano, e
nale d'Arte Lu
pografie, die
Arbeiten

Caramel hearts

Christmas is the best time to indulge your sweet tooth.
If someone you love is a fan of sweet hot drinks,
these sugar hearts are perfect.

Just add them to hot milk, coffee, or tea and enjoy! The ideal gift to take to an advent gathering.

How it's done:

1. Warm the sugar in a saucepan over medium heat until it melts. Don't put it over high heat or take your eyes off the pan, because the caramelized sugar burns easily. Children's hands have no business here.

2. When the caramel is light golden in color, remove the saucepan from the heat. Stir some cinnamon into the liquid caramel to give it a Christmassy flavor, if you like, but it also tastes great without this addition.

3. Pour the liquid mixture into the silicone mold and leave to cool. Do not touch hot caramel, however tempted you may be to have a taste!

✳ ❀ ❀
🕘 *30 minutes*

You will need:
* *1lb 2oz (500g) white granulated sugar (see below)*
* *saucepan*
* *1 tsp ground cinnamon, or to taste (optional)*
* *silicone heart mold*

✳ Tip ✳

It is vital to use white sugar here. Brown or light brown sugars won't caramelize.

Typography picture

*Letters have long been an interior design winner,
and who would guess it's so easy to produce your own fantastic,
customized typography design?*

∗∗❊

🕙 *about 1 hour per picture*

You will need:

∗ *graphite paper*
∗ *birch plywood panels, ½–¾in*
    (10–15mm) thick, 20 × 10in
    (50 × 25cm) and 8 × 8in
    (20 × 20cm)
∗ *templates (see p129)*
∗ *adhesive tape*
∗ *ballpoint pen*
∗ *black and anthracite acrylic paint*
∗ *flat paintbrush, ¾in (2cm) wide*
∗ *thin round paintbrush*

This monochrome look is not only totally on trend, it also works really well in most homes—but you can use colors if you prefer.

How it's done:

1. Lay the graphite paper with the coated side facing down onto a wooden panel. Place the template centrally on top and fix it in place with the tape.

2. Trace the contour of the typographical template with a ballpoint pen to copy the motif onto the panel.

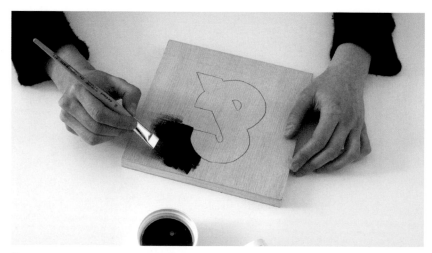

3. Now remove the template and paper and paint the wood with acrylic paint, either painting the letter or the area around it. Use a flat brush for large areas and a thin round brush for the finer work around the corners and edges.

Kitchen apron

*A great gift for the person making Christmas dinner,
or even for the reluctant cook who you want
to get involved in the kitchen.*

There's no reason why an apron shouldn't also look stylish. This is a lovely
present for anyone who likes to spend time in the kitchen cooking, baking,
or simply hanging out. And it's a simple sewing project for beginners.

How it's done:

1. Fold the fabric in half lengthwise, with right sides facing, and lay the
pattern along the fold. Pin the template in place on the fabric and trace the
outline using tailor's chalk or pencil. Cut out the apron and all 3 straps.

2. First sew the straps. To do this, fold in both the long edges, fix with pins,
and sew along both sides.

3. Now hem the apron. Fold the outer edge over twice by ½in (1cm), pin in
place, and sew. This works best if you start with the 2 arm sections (seam A
on the template), then sew along the sides (B), and finally the lower edge
of the apron. ➥

**❄

🕑 *1–2 hours*

You will need:

* *cotton fabric, 1½yd × 38in*
  (140 × 100cm)
* *pattern template (see p130)*
* *pins*
* *tailor's chalk, or pencil*
* *scissors*
* *sewing machine*
* *cotton thread*

For sewing tips and tricks, see p107.

4. After this, sew the straps onto the apron—first fold the open end of the long straps inward and sew. Then pin the straps on the reverse side of the apron at position F, and sew them on from the right side.

5. Fold over the top edge (C) twice, as you did before—the turnover here should be 1½in (3.5cm) wide.

6. Now you sew the neck strap onto the apron. Lay both ends of the loop that will go around the head under the turnover (G). Sew the lower seam (D) of the turnover, fixing the neck loop in place as you do this. Finally fold up the neck loop and sew the upper seam (E). This stitches the neck strap firmly in place for a second time.

"Give sincerely and freely. Bestow what dwells within you— your opinions, taste, and humor—and you will be abundantly rewarded."

Joachim Ringelnatz

* Tip *

To make the hemming easier here, iron all the edges and pin them in place before sewing.

Crunchy coffee-break cookies

Have you been invited to a festive coffee morning? Why not take along something you've baked?

These beautifully decorated cookies are not just delicious, they are also the perfect decorative gift for tea and coffee lovers.

How it's done:

1. Preheat the oven to 350°F (180°C). Line a baking sheet with parchment paper.

2. Put the flour, butter, sugar, egg, baking soda, vanilla, cocoa, and salt into a large bowl and knead together until you have a smooth dough.

3. Shape little balls from the dough, each slightly smaller than a walnut, then roll these between your hands to create a little roll. Bend the dough rolls into a U-shape and press the underside flat onto the work surface. Lay the cookies on the prepared sheet and bake for about 10 minutes until crisp. Leave to cool.

4. Now shape little rolls out of the fondant, bend them into a U-shape and flatten the base, then press them onto the flat underside of the cookies. Press chopped pistachios into the fondant.

∗∗❄

⊕ 2 hours, plus cooling time

You will need:
For the cookies:
* *2 cups (250g) all-purpose flour*
* *1 stick (125g) unsalted butter, softened*
* *¼ cup (90g) superfine sugar*
* *1 egg, lightly beaten*
* *¼ tsp baking soda*
* *½ tsp pure vanilla extract*
* *1 tsp cocoa powder*
* *pinch of salt*
* *½ cup (100g) white fondant*
* *3 tbsp (25g) chopped pistachios*

In addition:
* *baking sheet*
* *parchment paper*

Beaded sweater

There's no need to wear a necklace if your clothing is gently sparkling with translucent, pearly beads.

✱ ❋ ❋

🕐 *1 hour*

You will need:

* ✱ *beading needle*
* ✱ *thread in a suitable color*
* ✱ *glass wax beads, ¼in (4mm) diameter*
* ✱ *wool sweater*
* ✱ *scissors*

With just a few stitches, you can jazz up a simple sweater in festive fashion. Simply stitch on a few pretty beads and your Christmas top is ready—a really special present.

How it's done:

1. Using a beading needle and thread, sew pearly beads onto the sweater. Make sure to sew in the loose thread ends. If the beads are spaced no further than 1¼–1½in (3–4cm) apart, you can run the thread between them on the inside of the garment.

2. You can arrange the beads spaced out exactly as you please. We began at the top with lots of beads, then gradually spaced them out more widely farther down. We left the sleeves completely plain, but of course, the beads look absolutely lovely there, too, if you prefer.

Knitted slippers

***Slippers are a thoughtful and welcome gift, hugging the feet of
your loved ones and keeping them cosy and warm.***

Our knitted slippers are comfortable to wear, and also look great. They can be
for small and large feet. Give away, or keep for yourself! You will find tips and
tricks on knitting from page 110.

How it's done:

Gauge swatch: 17 stitches and 22 rows stockinette stitch, with the yarn
knitted double, 5mm (US size 8; UK size 6) needles = 4 × 4in (10 × 10cm).

The slippers are knitted with the yarn held double. If you have 2 balls of yarn,
knit with a strand from each ball. If you only have 1 ball, find the end of the
yarn in the center of the ball and knit this together with the thread coming
from the outside.

Both slippers are knitted identically, partially in stockinette stitch, partially
in garter stitch. Initially they are knitted back and forth, then in rounds on the
double-pointed needles. For the garter stitch selvedge, the edge stitches are
worked by slipping the first stitch knitwise at the start of each row; the final
stitch in each row is simply knitted. The details for the different sizes are
given in brackets: size 1 (size 2: size 3: size 4: size 5).➤➤

***

🕑 *1–4 hours per pair, depending
on size and knitting ability*

You will need:

* set of 8in (20cm) long 5mm (US size
8; UK size 6) double-pointed needles
* DK-weight yarn in 2 colors, here:
Lamana Cusco (100% alpaca),
quantity according to size:
  Size 1 *(Child size: US 10.5 11.5 / UK
27–29) (4–6 years, foot length about
7in / 17.5cm): about 93yd (50g)
color A, about 30yd (15g) color B*
  Size 2 *(Child size: US 12.5–1 / UK
30–32)(7–9 years, foot length about
7¾in / 19.5cm): about 186yd (100g)
color A, about 60yd (30g) color B*
  Size 3 *(Women size: US 5–6 / UK
35–36)(foot length about 8¾in /
22cm): about 186yd (100g) color A,
about 60yd (30g) color B*
  Size 4 *(Women size: US 7–8 / UK
38–39)(foot length about 9½in /
24cm): about 186yd (100g) color A,
about 60yd (30g) color B*
  Size 5 *(Women size: US 9–10 / UK
40–41)(foot length about 10½in /
26cm): about 242yd (130g) color A,
about 90yd (45g) color B*
* stitch marker
* scissors
* yarn needle

1. Cast on 26 (30:30:34:38) stitches loosely in color A with the yarn held double. The trailing yarn end should be about 10in (25cm) long, to allow you to use this to sew up the heel seam later.

2. 1st row (wrong side): slip 1, knit 4 (5:5:6:6), purl 16 (18:18:20:24), knit 5 (6:6:7:7), edge stitch.

3. 2nd row (right side): slip 1, knit to end.

4. Repeat the 1st and 2nd rows until, after about 20 (22:26:28:30) rows, the piece measures 3 (3½:4½:5:5¼) in (8 [9:11.5:12.5:13.5] cm).

5. From the next wrong side row, reduce the lateral garter stitch sections on every wrong side row as follows: slip 1, knit 3 (4:4:5:5), purl 18 (20:20:22:26), knit 4 (5:5:6:6), edge stitch.

6. Next right side row: slip 1, knit to end.

7. Next wrong side row: slip 1, knit 2 (3:3:4:4), purl 20 (22:22:24:28), knit 3 (4:4:5:5).

8. Next right side row: slip 1, knit to end.

9. Reduce the garter stitch section in this way until on a wrong side row, there is just 1 stitch knitted between the edge stitches at the start and end of the row, and the stitches in between are all purl stitches.

The piece should measure 4¼ (5:5½:6¼:7) in (11 [12.5:14:16:17.5] cm) and have 25 (29:33:37:39) rows.

10. On the next right side row, the stitches are distributed between 4 double-pointed needles. The 1st needle is always the beginning of a round. To help you count the rounds, place a stitch marker on needle 1. On needle 1, work the 1st decrease: knit 1, SKP (slip one (knitwise), knit 1, pass slipped stitch over). On needle 4, work the 2nd decrease: knit the second- and third-to-last stitches on the needle together. There should now be 6 (7:7:8:9) stitches on each needle.

11. On the 4th round (counting from the stitch marker on needle 1), switch to color B at the start of the 3rd needle. Cut the double strands of color A and continue to knit in rounds.

12. At the start of round 5 (5:5:6:6) in color B, begin decreasing for the toe (start on needle 1). To do this, work the 1st decrease on needles 1 and 3 and the 2nd decrease on needles 2 and 4. Work the decreases on every other round until there are 5 (4:4:5:5) stitches on every needle.

13. Now work the decreases on every round until there are 2 stitches on each needle for any size of slipper. Cut the double strands and use a yarn needle to pull these through the remaining stitches.

14. Turn the slipper inside side out and sew in the yarn carefully on the inside at the toe and at the color change.

15. Fold over the cast on edge (at the rear center) and close the heel seam neatly using the yarn you left hanging from when you cast on. Work the second slipper in exactly the same way.

"That which issues from the heart alone, will bend the hearts of others to your own."

Johann Wolfgang von Goethe

Wrapping

Beautifully wrapped gifts are not just fun to receive, but preparing them also adds to the excited anticipation of Christmas Day. The projects in this chapter show that original gift-wrapping ideas don't have to be a lot of work.

Merry Christmas

Festive gift wrap with paper bows

Creative gifts with a thoughtful and personal touch of detail are a particular joy to receive; at Christmas the wrapping paper is far more than just packaging.

Really special wrapping ideas don't have to involve lots of time or money. With just a few small steps and a bit of creativity, you can transform your presents into something so beautiful that no one will want to unwrap them!

How it's done:

1. Use a calligraphy pen to transform your handwriting and create a gift wrap design. Write out festive texts, such as poems or lyrics, in generously curved letters on the plain wrapping paper.

2. To make the pretty bow, use the template to cut both sections out of white paper. Dab a bit of glue in the center of section A and press both ends firmly on top. Then glue this bow centrally onto section B.

∗ ❋ ❋
🕐 *15 minutes*

You will need:
* ∗ *calligraphy pen*
* ∗ *plain wrapping paper*
* ∗ *bow template (see p131)*
* ∗ *scissors*
* ∗ *white paper*
* ∗ *glue stick*

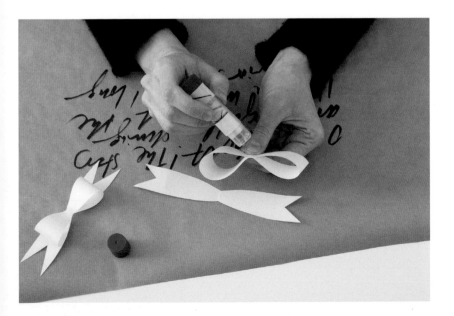

Ribbons

These pretty fabric ribbons add a homemade touch to any gift wrap, and they are quick and easy to make yourself from recycled fabric remnants.

✳ ❋ ❋

🕐 *5 minutes per ribbon, plus drying time*

You will need:

* ✳ *thin white cotton fabric*
* ✳ *scissors*
* ✳ *foil or paper to use as underlay*
* ✳ *wide, flat paintbrush*
* ✳ *silk paint in blue, pink, and green*
* ✳ *small drinking glass*
* ✳ *iron*

We tore fabric into long strips, then dyed it with silk paint to upcycle it into gift wrap ribbon.

How it's done:

1. Rip the cotton fabric into narrow strips. To do this, snip slightly into the material following the direction of the fabric grain, then tear down from this incision. You will get lovely evenly frayed edges.

2. Lay the fabric strips on your underlay and brush with water.

3. Dilute some silk paint with water in a small drinking glass, then brush the wet fabric strip with this so it has an even color.

4. Leave the fabric strip to dry, then fix the color with the iron, according to the silk dye package instructions.

Cookie gift tags

Do you have a horde of kids, great-grandmas, second cousins, and adopted "family" coming for Christmas this year? To avoid any mix-ups when the presents are handed out, the best idea is to attach homemade name tags to each.

These cookie tags are easy to bake and can be gobbled up as soon as the presents have been distributed.

How it's done:

1. Preheat the oven to 425°F (220°C). Line a baking sheet with parchment paper. In a large bowl, mix the flour, pudding mix, baking powder, sugar, ground almonds, salt, cinnamon, ginger, and vanilla.

2. Brown the butter in a small saucepan, then let it cool slightly.

3. Now add the butter, honey, and eggs to the bowl of dry ingredients and work everything together until you have a smooth, firm dough. Leave the dough to rest for 15 minutes in the fridge.

4. Dust a work surface with flour and roll the dough out thinly using a rolling pin. Stamp out individual cookies and use the letter stamp to print names in the cookies. Make a little hole in the dough at the top of each using a straw.

5. Place the cookies on the prepared baking sheet. Bake for around 10 minutes until they are golden brown, then leave to cool.

6. Finally, melt the chocolate ganache over a double boiler according to the manufacturer's instructions. Once it has completely melted, dip the lower half of each cookie into the chocolate. Let the chocolate coating solidify. You can attach the cookies to the presents using a little ribbon through the hole.

◀◀ *The paper gift tags can be found at the back of the book!*

** ❄
🕓 *2 hours, plus cooling time*

You will need:
For the cookies:
* ✦ *1¼ cups (300g) all-purpose flour*
* ✱ *1 packet of chocolate pudding mix*
* ✱ *2 tsp baking soda*
* ✱ *¾ cup (150g) superfine sugar*
* ✱ *¼ cup (75g) ground almonds*
* ✱ *pinch of salt*
* ✱ *pinch of ground cinnamon*
* ✱ *1 tsp ground ginger*
* ✱ *1 tsp pure vanilla extract*
* ✱ *1½ sticks (150g) unsalted butter*
* ✱ *1 tbsp honey*
* ✱ *2 eggs, lightly beaten*

In addition:
* ✱ *cookie cutters*
* ✱ *letter stamps*
* ✱ *straw*
* ✱ *½ cup (200g) chocolate ganache sauce, from cooking stores or online*
* ✱ *double boiler*
* ✱ *thin ribbon*

Envelopes for Christmas mail

Wherever your loved ones might be, Christmas is a chance to surprise them with a few handwritten words.

* ❄ ❄

🕐 *2 minutes per envelope*

You will need:

* *self-adhesive address labels*
* *colored envelopes*
* *glue stick*
* *copper-colored glitter*

After all, it's always lovely to get real mail, especially in this age of email. This project shows you how to design a special envelope to suit the occasion for your Christmas missive.

How it's done:

1. First stick an address label on a colored envelope in the position where the address will go later.

2. Use a glue stick to mark around the label, applying the glue evenly, so the glitter will adhere.

3. Now scatter some glitter onto the sticky surface, spreading it with your finger and pressing slightly. Shake the loose glitter off over the sink.

4. Finally, you just need to pull off the address label carefully to leave a clear, well-defined space in which to address the letter.

* Tip *

If the labels stick on too strongly and won't come off the envelopes, stick them onto a piece of fabric briefly beforehand. They will pick up little textile fibers that then prevent the label from sticking too firmly.

Rudolph gift wrap

Who's that peeking out at us? Rudolph! The friendly face with the famous red nose will particularly thrill young kids. This is a fun idea for a craft activity to brighten up the pre-Christmas period, too.

How it's done:

1. First wrap up your present in the brown wrapping paper. Copy the antler templates with a color photocopier and cut them out (or just make them out of brown paper).

2. To make the eyes, punch out a couple of circles from black paper using a hole punch. Stick them on using the glue stick. You could also cut out eyes by hand, or paint them.

3. Below the eyes, stick on the pom-pom as the nose. Use the craft knife to make a little slit in the gift wrap along the front edge where the antlers should go.

4. Fold over the ends of the antlers by about ½in (1cm), dab a bit of glue onto both sides of the folded-over ends, stick them into the slit in the paper, and press them into place.

* ❄ ❄
🕑 *5 minutes per present*

You will need:
* *brown wrapping paper*
* *templates (see pp132–133)*
* *scissors*
* *black paper*
* *hole punch*
* *glue stick*
* *1 red pom-pom per present, ½–¾in (1–2cm) in diameter*
* *craft knife*

Gift bags

A lovely packaging idea to wrap small presents for coworkers, friends at school, the mail carrier, and all those other wonderful people whose Christmas you want to brighten up a little.

✱✱❀

🕐 *15 minutes to make the transfer, 2 minutes for printing each bag*

You will need:

⁎ *scissors*
⁎ *template (see pp134–135)*
⁎ *linoleum block*
⁎ *pencil*
⁎ *linoleum cutters*
⁎ *acrylic paint*
⁎ *craft paper*
⁎ *linoleum ink roller or brayer*
⁎ *paper bags*

How it's done:

1. Cut out the template and transfer the shape onto the linoleum using the pencil. Use the linoleum cutter to carve out the lines that shouldn't be printed (these are printed black on the template). Be careful when using the cutting tool to work away from your body, moving the linoleum rather than the tool, so you don't cut yourself. Finally, cut out the heart shape itself.

2. Put some acrylic paint onto a piece of craft paper. Roll out the paint with the ink roller until the roller is coated. When the roller is evenly covered with paint, transfer the paint onto the linoleum heart.

3. As soon as the linoleum has been evenly covered in the paint, print the shape onto a paper bag.

Money crackers

At first sight, giving money might not seem particularly creative, but this wrapping makes each note unique.

These homemade Christmas crackers can be individually designed and are a lot prettier than an envelope. You can also fill the crackers with confetti, charms for good luck, or homemade sayings for a New Year's Eve party.

How it's done:

1. Shape 1 of the thick pieces of paper into a little tube with a diameter of roughly 1¼in (3cm). Fix the tube in place using a piece of tape, then stuff a dollar bill inside.

2. Spread some glue along one side of this paper tube.

3. Lay the paper tube along a short end of the tissue paper sheet so that it sticks in place. Now roll up the paper tube inside the tissue paper, and glue the edge in place.

4. Tie up the cracker on both sides with the colored thread. Finally, cut both ends of the cracker so they are the same length.

★ ❋ ❋
🕐 *5 minutes per cracker*

You will need:

* *sheets of craft paper, 5 × 3in (14 × 6.5cm)*
* *adhesive tape*
* *glue stick*
* *1 8½ × 11in sheet of white tissue paper per cracker*
* *colorful thread*
* *scissors*
* *1 dollar bill for each cracker*

Wenn wir im Traume ...
alle unfeindlich sind,
uns alle Kinder sind.
Wie es sein soll, wie ...
Joachim Ringelnatz

Gift voucher balls

If you want to give someone a gift voucher, these transparent balls are a particularly pretty way to present them.

The balls can be stuffed with a personal message or seasonal quotation, then hung on the tree until the moment that presents are handed out and they give up their secrets.

How it's done:

1. Cut the paper to an appropriate size for your ornament. Ours measure 3in (7.5cm) in diameter, so we cut our gift voucher slips to roughly 3 × 2in (8 × 5cm). Write your message on the paper.

2. Carefully remove the hanging mount from the ornament, roll up the paper with the writing facing outward, and insert this into the ornament so it can be read through the ornament.

∗ ❋ ❋

🕐 *10 minutes per ornament*

You will need:

∗ *scissors*
∗ *paper*
∗ *pen, ideally a calligraphy pen*
∗ *transparent tree ball with removable hanging mount*

3. Replace the hanging mount… and you're done.

∗ Tip ∗

If the gift voucher is too big, it will either not fit in the ornament at all, or it won't unfurl. It should be legible when it is inside the ornament.

Last-minute ideas

✦

*Has Christmas suddenly crept up on you
this year? No problem! With these quick ideas,
you can conjure up something festive
in no time at all.*

Decorating

Candle bottles

These beautiful candlesticks bring a festive mood to your home, and can be made in just a few minutes.

Long candles take center stage with the help of a couple of pretty, aromatic sprigs from different types of evergreen and some decorative glass bottles. What's more, your house will have a beautiful woodland and wintry scent. A great idea for rapidly conjuring up a Christmassy atmosphere.

How it's done:

1. If necessary, first trim the sprigs to the size of the bottles, then insert them inside the individual bottles. We used sprigs from pine, fir, box, and holly.

2. Finally, twist the candle into the neck of the bottle. To make sure it stands firmly in place, warm the wax at the bottom of the candle first.

∗ ❄ ❄

🕑 *10 minutes*

You will need:

∗ *pruning shears*
∗ *various sprigs of evergreen foliage*
∗ *empty glass bottles*
∗ *candles*

"I will honor Christmas in my heart, and try to keep it all the year."

Charles Dickens

∗ Tip ∗

If your candles are prone to dripping, make sure you put something underneath to catch the melted wax.

Wrapping

Wooden boxes

These lovely and exceptionally practical round boxes can be found in any well-stocked craft store.

* ❄ ❄

🕐 *1–5 minutes per box*

You will need:

* * *wooden boxes*
* * *acrylic paint in various colors*
* * *paintbrush*
* * *masking tape in gold and silver*

By adding a bit of color, these containers can quickly be transformed into personalized gift boxes. There is no way these will be thrown away—they can simply be reused again and again. Here we've used our boxes for cookies and delicious baked treats, but of course they are just as good for jewelry or whatever gift you want to put inside. The boxes also stack nicely, and so are an ideal storage system for all your essential little bits and pieces.

How it's done:

1. Paint the wooden boxes using acrylic paint in whatever colors you like—we used black, white, red, and yellow. You can paint them inside or outside, maybe just the lid, the same color all over, or multicolored.

2. Festive masking tape—in gold or silver or other bright colors—makes a lovely decoration for the edge of the lid.

"The manner of giving is worth more than the gift."

Pierre Corneille

Decorating

Floating candles

This table decoration can be made in the twinkling of an eye. It is wonderfully festive as well as having a modern look, and you can coordinate the color of the water to match your table setting.

The floating lights guarantee a relaxed atmosphere and a cozy mood at the table. What's more, you don't need to worry about the decoration catching fire, as it is already in water.

How it's done:

1. Fill the glass containers with water. Make sure the water levels vary.

2. Now add a couple of drops of color to the water and mix to combine evenly.

3. Finally, float the candles on the water, putting 1 or more into each container before lighting them.

∗ ❄ ❄
🕙 *10 minutes*

You will need:

∗ *various glass containers*
∗ *food coloring, watercolors, silk paint, or ink*
∗ *floating candles*

∗ Tip ∗

Make sure you buy floating candles that burn for a long time, otherwise you will have to keep replacing them.

Giving
Bath salts

Bath salts are a lovely present for all those stressed-out people in the world… someone you love will probably needs these!

This is a pampering gift which, in a sense, grants the recipient permission to give themselves a bit of "me" time. After all that Christmas stress, a hot bath ensures a strong dose of relaxation and recovery.

How it's done:

1. Mix the bath salts with a few dried rose petals and/or lavender flowers (use a proportion of roughly 1 handful of bath salts to 1 tsp petals) and put the mixture into a screw top jar.

2. Tie raffia around the jar. Cover the lid with brown paper. Transfer the star template onto the silver colored paper, cut out the star, and stick this on the lid.

✱ ❊ ❊
🕐 *5 minutes*

You will need:
* *natural bath salts with no added substances*
* *dried rose petals and/ or lavender flowers*
* *teaspoon*
* *screw top jar*
* *raffia*
* *brown paper*
* *template (see p122)*
* *silver colored paper*
* *scissors*
* *all-purpose glue*

✱ Tip ✱

Take care to avoid getting the bath salts wet, so they don't clump together.

"The enigma of Christmas is that, on our quest for the great and the extraordinary, our attention is drawn to the inconsequential and the small."

Author unknown

Giving

Lavender bags

These fragrant and pretty pouches are the ideal little gift next time you are invited over by friends or family.

The lavender bags can be kept in your closet among your winter sweaters and coats to protect the clothes from moth damage. At the same time, they fill the closet with a lovely aroma.

How it's done:

1. Cut the fabric for each bag into a 11 × 4in (28 × 10cm) shape. Fold the piece widthwise in the middle and sew up the sides (for tips on sewing, see pp107–109).

2. Now turn the bag, easing out the corners using the tips of the scissors, and fill with dried lavender flowers.

3. Finally, tie the bag at the top with a piece of lace trim.

∗ ❈ ❈

🕓 *5 minutes per bag*

You will need:

* *scissors*
* *white linen fabric, 11 × 4in (28 × 10cm) for each bag*
* *white thread*
* *sewing machine*
* *dried lavender flowers*
* *lace trim, 10in (25cm) for each bag*

∗ Tip ∗

If you are not a fan of the scent of lavender, you could also fill the bags with dried cloves or cinnamon sticks.

Wrapping

Apple cards

Beautiful notes that come from the heart don't have to be expensive—just really personal. A simple apple, plus a bit of red paint, and your Christmas card is ready to send!

∗ ❋ ❋

🕐 *1 minute per card*

You will need:
∗ *knife*
∗ *apple*
∗ *red acrylic paint*
∗ *small sponge*
∗ *white cards and envelopes*

The most memorable presents are little handmade gifts. Although this project is simple, the printed card is a one-off and far nicer, we think, than store-bought Christmas cards. The kids will love helping out with this project, too!

How it's done:

1. Cut the apple lengthwise through the middle.

2. Dab the cut surfaces with paint using the little sponge, and use it as a stamp to decorate the cards and envelopes.

3. Leave to dry, write a heartfelt message… then put it in the mail!

🔔

The apple is the predecessor of the Christmas tree ornament. As early as medieval times, trees would have been decorated with apples to represent the tree of life, from the biblical Garden of Eden. Later additions included lebkuchen (see p32) and nuts. After Twelfth Night, from January 6, all the tree decorations could be eaten!

Techniques & templates

Sewing

These sewing techniques will help you with
the projects on pages 42, 46, 62, and 102.

Simple basting stitch

You work from right to left. Start with a knot on the end of a thread, thread the needle, then poke the needle in and out of the material at regular intervals.

Sewing machine straight stitch

Most modern sewing machines can sew a variety of utility and decorative stitches, as well as buttonholes. Straight stitch is suitable for most purposes. The stitch length can usually be adjusted up to ¼in (5mm).

Buttonhole stitch

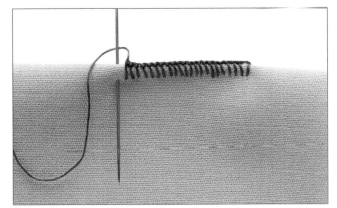

1. Sew narrow stitches from right to left over the edge of the fabric. The needle should come down vertically through the edge of the fabric.

2. Arrange the thread behind the upper end of the needle and underneath the tip of the needle. When you pull the needle through, a knot will be created at the edge of the material to form a neat border effect.

Embroidery

These embroidery techniques will help with the project on page 26.

Running stitch

This simplest stitch of all can be used on any type of needlework project.

1. Take the needle in and out of the fabric along the line being stitched. Keep the stitch length even on top. Short stitches on the back will make the front stitches closer together, and vice versa.

Backstitch

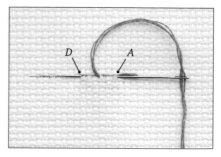

Backstitch creates a straight line without the spacing of running stitch.

1. Work from right to left. Bring the needle out at A, one stitch length from the right-hand end of the guideline. Insert it at B, the end of the line. Come out at C, one stitch length in front of A.

2. Insert at A again, and come out at D. Continue along the line.

Cross-stitch

A single cross-stitch is formed by two stitches crossing each other at an angle.

1. Bring the needle up on the base line at A and work one diagonal stitch to B, from bottom right to upper left.

2. Bring the needle up on the base line at C directly below the end of the first diagonal stitch.

3. To finish the cross, work another diagonal stitch to D, across the first one, in the opposite direction.

Row cross-stitch

To work a row of neat cross-stitches, keep the top and base of the stitch the same number of rows apart.

1. Work evenly spaced diagonal stitches in one direction to the end of the row.

2. Bring the needle up on the base line directly below the end of the last diagonal stitch. Work back in the opposite direction, making a row of diagonal stitches that crosses the first row.

Straight stitch

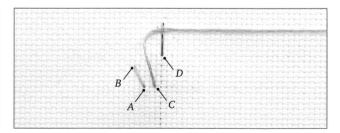

Also called stroke stitch or single satin stitch. The length, slant, and regularity can vary, but keep the stitching fairly short.

1. Bring the needle out at A and insert at B. Come out at C and insert at D. Repeat.

Knitting

These knitting techniques will help you with the projects on pages 46 and 70.

Single cast on

1. Hold the needle with the slip knot in your right hand. Place the yarn, as shown, around your left thumb and hold it with your other fingers. Then take the needle around the thread in the direction shown by the arrow.

2. Let the yarn slip off your thumb and pull the yarn to tighten the new cast on loop on the needle, sliding it up close to the slip knot.

3. Loop the yarn around your thumb again and repeat this process until you have as many stitches on the needle as required.

Knitted cast on

1. Place the needle with the slip knot on it in the left hand. Insert the tip of the right needle from right to left through the center of the loop on the left needle, as shown.

2. With the yarn behind the needles, wrap it under and around the tip of the right needle. While casting on, use the left index finger or middle finger to hold the loops on the left needle in position.

3. With the tip of the right needle, carefully draw the yarn through the loop on the left needle. This is the same way that knit stitch is formed.

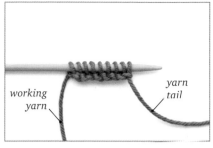

4. Transfer the loop on the right needle to the left needle by inserting the tip of the left needle from right to left through the front of the loop.

5. Pull both yarn ends to tighten the new cast on loop on the needle, sliding it up close to the slip knot.

6. Continue in this way until you have the required number of stitches.

working yarn

yarn tail

Knit stitch

1. Hold the needle with the unworked stitches in your left hand and the other needle in your right hand. With the working yarn behind the needle, insert the right needle from left to right through the center of the next stitch to be worked on the left needle.

2. Wrap the yarn under and around the tip of the right needle, keeping an even tension on the yarn as it slips through your fingers.

3. Catch the yarn with the tip of the right needle and carefully draw it through the stitch on the left needle. Try to hold the yarn firmly, but not too tightly.

4. Let the old loop drop off the left needle to complete the stitch. Work all the stitches on the left needle onto the right needle in the same way to complete the row. Turn the work and transfer the right needle to the left hand.

Purl stitch

1. Hold the free working needle in your right hand. With the working yarn at the front of the knitting, insert the tip of the right needle from right to left through the center of the next stitch to be worked on the left needle.

2. Wrap the yarn over and around the tip of the right needle. Try to keep an even tension on the yarn as you release the yarn through your fingers.

3. With the tip of the right needle, carefully draw the yarn through the stitch on the left needle. Keep your hands relaxed and allow the yarn to slip through your fingers in a gently controlled manner.

4. Let the old loop drop off the left needle to complete the stitch. Work all the stitches on the left needle onto the right needle in the same way to complete the row. To start the next row, turn the work and transfer the knitting to the left hand.

Garter stitch

1. Garter stitch is worked entirely in knit stitch. The right and wrong sides look the same. When the right side of the fabric is facing you, knit all the stitches in the row.

2. When the wrong side of the fabric is facing you, knit all the stitches in the row. The resulting fabric is soft, textured, and slightly stretchy with edges that lie flat.

Stockinette stitch

1. Stockinette stitch is formed by working a row of knit stitches and a row of purl stitches alternately. When the right side of the fabric is facing you, as shown, knit all the stitches in the row.

2. When the wrong side of the fabric is facing you, as shown, purl all the stitches in the row. The wrong side is often referred to as the "purl side" of the knitting.

Gauge swatch

Before beginning any knitting project, you should make a gauge swatch. Depending how loosely or tightly you knit, you may need to use a different needle size in order to achieve the gauge required by the pattern.

1. Using the specified needle size, knit a swatch about 5in (13cm) square. Mark 4in (10cm) across the center of your swatch with pins and count the number of stitches between the pins.

2. Count the number of rows to 4in (10cm) in the same way. If you have fewer stitches and rows than you should, try again with a smaller needle size; if you have more, change to a larger needle size. Use the needle size for your knitting that best matches the correct tension given for your pattern.

Knit 2 stitches together

1. Insert the tip of the right needle from left to right through the second stitch, then the first stitch on the left needle.

2. Wrap the yarn around the tip of the right needle, draw the yarn through both loops, and drop the old stitches off the left needle.

3. This makes two stitches into one and decreases one stitch in the row. The completed stitch slants right.

Knitting with five double-pointed needles

1. Cast on your stitches on a single needle, then distribute them across 4 double-pointed needles. Insert a stitch marker between the first 2 stitches on the first round. Arrange the needles to form a square, making sure not to twist your cast on row.

2. You knit with the free, fifth needle. Knit the first stitch on each needle tightly to avoid gaps at the point where you transition from 1 needle to another.

3. When the stitches on the first needle have all been knitted, this becomes your working needle. Continue to knit in rounds, slipping the stitch marker from the left to right needle when it is reached.

Knitting in moss stitch

Cast on an even number of stitches. On the right side, work knit 1, purl 1, alternating; on the wrong side, work purl 1, knit 1, again alternating. If you have an uneven number of stitches, you should simply knit 1, purl 1 on all rows to make sure that you always end with a knit stitch.

Knitting with multiple colors
Two-color garter stitch stripe

This narrow stripe pattern is worked in garter stitch in two colors. To work the stripe, knit 2 rows in each color alternately, dropping the color not in use at the side of the work and picking it up again when it is needed.

Clean edges

When working two colored, even row stripes, twist the yarn around each other every ½–¾in (1–2cm) up the side of the piece. Alternating the direction of the twist after each color change prevents the yarns from becoming tangled. Be careful not to pull them tightly or the edge will pucker. This technique may make a bulky seam if used with more than two colors.

Weaving in the yarn ends

1. On right side rows it is possible to weave in ends as you knit. Start with the new color held in the right hand, and the old color over the left index finger. Insert the right needle into the first stitch. Bring the old color around front of right needle from right to left.

2. Bring the new color between the needles and knit the stitch as normal. By doing this, the old color yarn slips to the right and over the tip of the right needle, so it is not caught up as part of the new stitch. On the next stitch, don't knit in the old yarn.

3. Repeat steps 1 and 2 until the old yarn end has been firmly secured. Knit until finished, then snip the yarn ends. Leave around ½in (1cm) hanging so that the ends don't slip through to the right side and become visible.

Crocheting

These crochet techniques will help you with the project on page 54.

Chain stitch

A foundation chain (also known as an initial chain) made of chain stitches forms the basis of every crocheted item. Chain stitches are also needed for turning. In conjunction with other stitches, they produce a diverse range of open or closed stitch structures.

Chain stitch foundation chain

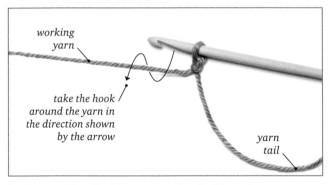

working yarn

take the hook around the yarn in the direction shown by the arrow

yarn tail

1. Start with a slip knot on your hook. Wrap the yarn around the hook. To do this, take the hook under the yarn and simultaneously pull the yarn slightly forward.

draw a loop through in the direction of the arrow

2. With the yarn caught in the tip of the hook, draw a loop of yarn through the loop on the hook shaft. Hold the base of the slip knot with the free fingers of your hand as you draw the loop through.

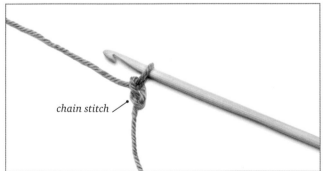

chain stitch

3. This completes the first chain stitch.

front of the chain stitch foundation chain

4. For each additional stitch, repeat and pull another loop through the stitch on the needle. Continue in this way until you have crocheted the specified number of chain stitches.

Counting chain stitches

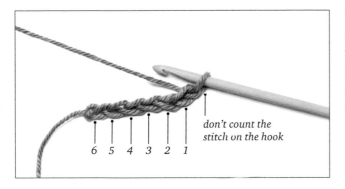

don't count the stitch on the hook

6 5 4 3 2 1

Count along as you crochet until the desired number of chain stitches has been reached. Before you continue with your project, it's a good idea to check your numbers again. Hold the foundation chain with the right side toward you and count the stitches from the crochet hook to the left.

Single crochet

Single crochet is often used—either on its own or in combination with other stitches.

When single crochet is worked back and forth in rows, it looks identical on both sides. If you work in rounds, the front and back of the work look different.

1. Crochet a foundation chain (see left) of the required length. Insert your hook through the second stitch from the hook and wrap the yarn around the hook following the arrow. Here the hook is inserted under a single strand, but you can also take the hook under 2 strands of yarn.

2. Hold the base of the foundation chain firmly in your left hand. Hold the yarn taut and draw a loop back through the chain stitch in the direction shown by the arrow. ➽

3. Now there are 2 loops on the crochet hook. Take the hook around the yarn in the direction shown by the arrow.

4. Pull the yarn loop through both stitches on the hook in one smooth action. Let the working yarn slide through your fingers, but keep the yarn tension constant.

5. The first single crochet stitch is complete. The skipped chain stitch at the start of the row is not counted as a stitch, it serves as a turning stitch.

6. Work a single crochet stitch in each of the following chain stitches in the row in exactly the same way.

7. At the end of the row, turn the work so that the working yarn lies to the right. You can then begin the next row.

8. At the start of the second row, crochet a chain stitch. This is the turning stitch. It takes the yarn up to the correct level for the next row of single crochet stitches.

9. Work the first single crochet into the top of the first stitch in the row below. Work a single crochet into the top of each remaining single crochets in the row below.

10. At the end of the row, work the last stitch into the top of the last single crochet of the row below. Work the following rows as for the second row.

11. When your piece is finished, cut the yarn, leaving a 4in (10cm) thread hanging. Remove the hook from the final stitch, bring the yarn end through, and pull the stitch firmly closed. This finishing technique is used for all stitch types.

Gauge swatch

Before beginning a crochet project, make a gauge swatch. Depending on how loosely or tightly you crochet, you may need to use a different hook size to achieve the tension specified in the pattern.

1. Using the specified hook, crochet a sample piece measuring about 5in (13cm) square. Insert 2 pins 4in (10cm) apart and count the stitches in between.

2. Count the rows over 4in (10cm) in the same manner. If there are fewer than specified in the pattern, try again with a slightly smaller crochet hook. If there are more, use a larger hook. Precision in the stitch width is more important than row height.

Single crochet increases

1. To increase one stitch at the beginning of a row of single crochet, work one single crochet stitch into the first stitch in the usual way. Next, insert the hook again into the first stitch and work a second single crochet in the same stitch.

2. This completes the increase. Proceed as usual, single crocheting into each single crochet stitch in the previous row. ➤➤

3. At the end of the row, work one single crochet stitch into the last stitch of the row in the usual way. Insert the hook again into the crochet stitch of the row and work a second single crochet stitch.

4. This increases one stitch at the end of the row.

Crocheting in the round using a loop

This crocheted loop is a quick and simple starting technique for flat shapes crocheted in the round. It lets you control the hole in the center.

1. Form a loop from the yarn and pull the working thread through.

2. Don't pull the loop closed. To begin the first round, crochet a chain stitch into the loop.

pull to close ring

3. Work the first round of single crochet stitches, working them into the ring and over the yarn tail as shown by the arrow.

4. When all of the required stitches are worked into the ring, pull the yarn tail to close the ring. Then continue as explained in the pattern instructions.

Pom-poms and tassels

*These pom-poms and tassels are needed for the projects
on pages 28 and 42.*

1. In both cases, first you wrap the yarn around a small, strong piece of paper. We used a business card. It's the ideal size.

2. To produce a tassel, you tie together the loops on 1 side of the card. To create a pom-pom, you tie together the loops on both sides of the card.

3. Slide the loops off the card. For the tassel (pink) you wrap a thread around all the loops just below where the ends are tied, bundling them together. This produces a little round "top knot."

4. For a pom-pom (red) you knot together the thread ends on both sides.

5. Finally, for both the tassel and the pom-pom, you cut the loops of yarn at the bottom and neatly trim the threads to the correct length.

You can download all the templates from our website www.supercraftlab.com/downloads

Decorating

Christmas tree decorations: painted wooden disks

Template for the projects on pages 30, 38, and 100.

Snowflake tablecloth

Template for the project on page 26.
You will find embroidery tips on pages 108–109.

Giving

Advent calendar

Templates for the project on page 38.

Enlarge all templates by 150%, or to your required size.

Good luck angel

Templates for the project on page 42.

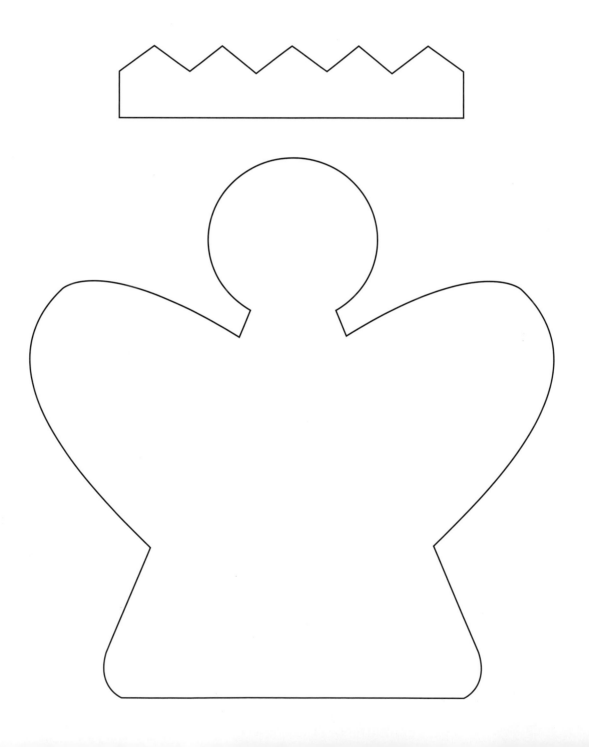

Cosmetic bags

Pattern for the project on page 48.

Enlarge template by 150%. Note that the ¾in (2cm) seam allowance is **not** taken into account in this pattern and will need to be added when cutting out the lining material.

Family T-shirts

Templates for the project on page 50.
Enlarge all templates by 170%.

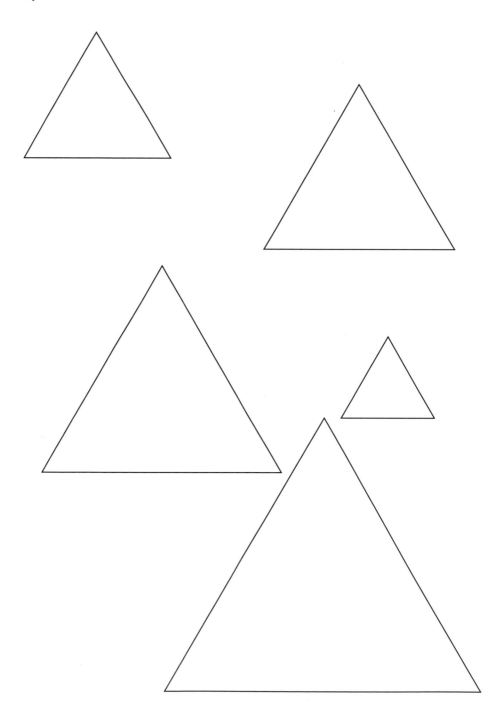

Typography picture

Templates for the project on page 60.

Enlarge all templates by 160%, or to your required size.

Kitchen apron

Pattern for the project on page 62.
Enlarge all templates by 475%.

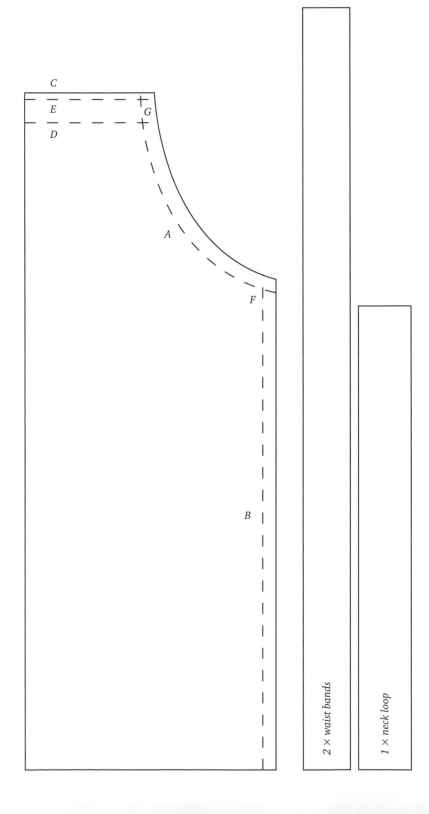

Packing

Festive gift wrap with paper bows

Templates for the project on page 76.
Enlarge all templates by 180%.

B

A

Rudolph gift wrap

Templates for the project on page 84.

Gift bags

Templates for the project on page 86.

Manufacturers & suppliers

When selecting our materials we focus particularly on quality and on fair manufacturing conditions and, wherever possible, we support small businesses. Many of the materials and tools used in this book come from friendly labels or established wholesalers with whom we also love working. The following links will help you track down suppliers and buy any required materials online.

Do-it-yourself kits, fabric, paper, paints, craft supplies: **www.michaels.com**
Yarn: **www.yarn.com**
Bakers twine: **www.thetwinery.com**
Art supplies: **www.dickblick.com**
Do-it-yourself accessories: **www.acehardware.com**
Needlework supplies: **www.stitchery.com**
Home improvement and furniture: **www.lowes.com**

About the authors

Sophie Pester and Catharina Bruns are the founders of Supercraft, the DIY kits and materials shop for creative crafting enthusiasts. Not only are they both passionate designers and crafters, they are also entrepreneurs and authors who are particularly involved in two related topics: do-it-yourself and entrepreneurship or, in other words, creative self-sufficiency. Their "hello handmade" project is one of the most popular design markets in Germany. They founded Lemon Books, which is a design platform and manufacturing initiative for creating personalized notebooks, and they also launched the interview and workshop series "superwork." Behind all these initiatives there is one overriding goal—they want to inspire people to discover their own creative powers and self-sufficiency and give them the courage to do more themselves—whether that's handicraft hobbies or launching their own business.

www.supercraftlab.com
www.hello-handmade.com
www.lemonbooks.de
www.super-work.com
www.workisnotajob.com

Other books by the authors:
Supercraft—easy projects for every weekend also published by DK
Work is not a job—Was Arbeit ist, entscheidest du! and *Frei sein statt frei haben. Mit den eigenen Ideen in die kreative berufliche Selbstständigkeit*, both published by Campus

Acknowledgments

Thank you, dear readers, for choosing our book! We hope our ideas spur on your imaginations and provide you with plenty of inspiration for a creative Christmas.

Of course, we give special thanks to our many helpers, without whom this book would never have been so wonderful. Our sincere thanks go to:

* Sophie's dearest goddaughter Philippa Renz
* Sophie's best friend Susan Renz
* Our dear friends: Tom Sonntag, Ulrike Dix, and Patrick Sonntag
* Our crochet and knitting expert and kind supporter Christel Meyer
* Our supporter and expert sewer Ursula Heinrich
* The creative florist Bianca Pechstein
* Sophie's parents Ulrike and Andreas Pester for the lovely shooting location, the pretty Christmas decorative scene, delicious catering, and moral support
* Sophie's granny Christel Dittrich for her moral support

A massive thank you to our favorite photographer Anne Deppe (**www.annedeppe.de**) and to DK publishers, particularly to our editor Katharina May, for a fabulous collaboration.

Photography Anne Deppe
Editor Julia Niehaus
Designer Daniela Rudolf

For DK Germany
Publisher Monika Schlitzer
Managing Editor Caren Hummel
Project Manager Katharina May
Production Manager Dorothee Whittaker
Production Coordinator Arnika Marx
Production Christine Rühmer

For DK UK
Translator Alison Tunley
Editor Lucy Bannell
Senior Editor Kathryn Meeker
Senior Art Editor Glenda Fisher
Producer, Preproduction Catherine Williams
Senior Producer Stephanie McConnell
Creative Technical Support Sonia Charbonnier
Managing Editor Stephanie Farrow
Managing Art Editor Christine Keilty
Americanizer Jenny Siklos
U.S. Consultant Jennifer Wendell Kosek
U.S. Editor Kayla Dugger
U.S. Managing Editor Lori Hand

First American Edition, 2017
Published in the United States by DK Publishing
345 Hudson Street, New York, New York 10014

Copyright © 2016 Dorling Kindersley Verlag GmbH
Text copyright © 2016 Sophie Pester and Catherina Bruns
Photography copyright © 2016 Anne Deppe,
with the exception of pp.107–20, which are © Dorling Kindersley Limited
Translation copyright © 2017 Dorling Kindersley Limited
DK, a Division of Penguin Random House LLC
18 19 20 21 10 9 8 7 6 5 4 3 2
004–305984–Sept/2017

A catalog record for this book is available from the Library of Congress.
ISBN 978-1-4654-6326-5

DK books are available at special discounts when purchased in bulk for sales promotions, premiums,
fund-raising, or educational use. For details, contact: DK Publishing Special Markets,
345 Hudson Street, New York, New York 10014 SpecialSales@dk.com

Printed and bound in China

A WORLD OF IDEAS:
SEE ALL THERE IS TO KNOW
www.dk.com

31901064544499